"Broken Places"

"Broken Places"

A Poetical Journey

Poetessa

NATALINA RUSSO

To order additional copies of this book, contact:
Xlibris Corporation
1-888-795-4274
www.Xlibris.com
Orders@Xlibris.com
38964

CONTENTS

Dedication

To my sons, Jo Jo and Frankie, for such
love, support and continuous
encouragement in reminding me of who
I am and my worthiness. My sons—my
true "Trophies" in life—Thank you!

Because of you, I live and I love.
Because of you, I smile once again.

Perhaps Strength Doesn't Reside
In Having Never Been Broken
But In The Courage Required
To Grow Strong In
The "Broken Places"

Natalina's poetry focuses on images and thoughts using metaphors and symbolism with exquisite word painting.

Milt Anderson
Author, Abuse of Power

I applaud Natalina's courage! The truth in her words will inspire any reader.

Kristen Jongen
Soul Soup

In Broken Places, Natalina Russo gives us a heartfelt poetry of love, motherhood, family, and faith.

Stephen Murabito
Author of Communion of Asiago

Natalina's poems offer a message to connect (Midnight Screams) comfort, heal (A Reflection of Me) and give hope (Cyprus Sunshine) to persons experiencing and overcoming the tragedies of life.

Carolyn Holland,
counselor. photo/journalist, author and
Facilitator of the Beanery Writers Group of Pittsburgh,
Pa

Forward

Broken Places, a poetry collection by Natalina Russo, brings to the reading world a heartfelt and pensive body of poems about relationships, family, travel and faith. Born in Italy and deeply appreciative of her Italian heritage, Natalina Russo became a U.S. citizen at 18 and remains a teacher and translator of Italian, as well as a professional journalist and real estate businesswoman, among other achievements. Mother of two sons, and a loving daughter to a warmly "Italian mother," she is also a woman with a passion for writing.

The collection provides testimony to many and profound changes in the world of poetry. Long ago in Colonial America poetry held a broad place in everyday life. Colonial newspapers abounded with poetry, and poems were often written as gifts to court a sweetheart, to decorate a vase or a needlework cushion, or to commemorate a moving public event or special private moment. The local clergyman often wrote as a means of exploring and conveying his faith, and a traveler became a poet to record extraordinary experience.

In later years, the place of poetry declined to something bookish and often inaccessible to the public sensibility, often relegated to college courses and very small sections in the corner bookshop, and sometimes to the vague mental wanderings or protests of a youthful bohemian existence. Today poetry is again broadening to become a widely-appreciated celebration of expression. Poetry journals and small presses have burgeoned in the publishing world. Technology has played a key role, as well, offering numerous opportunities for poets to share their work and listen to others' voices, too.

Broken Places is a poetry collection that arises out of this passion for the word and instinct for expression. Its pages are full of the reflection and feeling of the inner life and partake of the renewed conviction that we can write and should write. We have a song to sing, as birds sing on a summer day from a tiptop limb and dogs bark beneath the stars on a chill winter night. They are talking to the world around them, always with perfect faith that the word belongs to all of us, writers and listeners alike, united in the love of song.

L. W. van Keuren
Author and Associate Professor of English
California University of Pennsylvania

Acknowledgements

To expose my inner most feelings and deepest thoughts. To be vulnerable is my purpose, my gift to the world. Sharing my pain is the beauty of God within me. In sharing myself, my courage, my strength, my healing, I can ease the pain of others. I cherish the presence of all the people in my world. I would like to thank everyone who helped make this book a reality

Susan Phillips, for her artistic gift in capturing the true essence of my poetry within the woman (Jacket Cover Design)

To *Kristen Jongen*, for her expressions of beauty within her designs that inspires my soul . . . for her use of art and lyrics of "Strength to Go on" that touched me so

Hermaine Muno, and Marcia Sacco for bringing my longhand writing up to the 21st Century and also their editing skills

Rosselle Fabrez, Lisa Fernandez and Kate Philips from Xlibris Publishing for all their help in making this book a reality.

My sweet Italian mother, *Concettina*, and beautiful sisters, *Annette* and *Maryann*, for their continuous encouragement and support in convincing me to share my poetry with the world

Tanti Grazie to my uncle *Francesco Amato*, a well-known author and publisher throughout Europe, for his successful writings and poetry. May his spirit stay with me and guide me always

Professor Luise van Keuren, for her forward and educational enlightenment into the world of poetry

And, much love and gratitude for my two sons, *R. Joseph and Francesco,* for always believing in me

Rose of Flesh and of Blood

Such a Sight
When the moon hides behind the highest mountains
and disappears darkness falls

I am then left here alone
A vision so wonderful but so empty

To me your presence was that of a Rose
And from your flesh and blood came The Pain of Death

Do not feel sad for me my Love
For my hands are left empty without you

For I have been gifted once
I have eaten from your hands and shared your bread of life

Now that you are gone
I am left with the Rose
And the memories of your Flesh and of your Blood

New Horizon

In the morn I arise so clearly
In the depth of the morning dew

I feel a new horizon
The me I lost in you

I feel the strength upon me
As a mighty winded tide

I know a new beginning
Emerge from deep inside

I look at life so clearly now
Hope within my soul

I look for a new beginning
As a new tomorrow grows

No more will I be burdened
of thoughts from yesteryear

Looking forward to a new beginning
with much happier tears

Unrecognized Flower

Living in the shell of the night
Such a bitter time

I am an unrecognized flower
Feelings so weak throughout
So very, very weak

The blame within myself flourishes over and over
The Loss, my Blame

So I with you shall never return
Here I will leave my heart

Such a sadden person
You, stay always within my soul

I a miserable being
My tears flow as a flooded landscape
Remembering, Searching

Oh the time I met you
Now in the shell of the night

I struggle within the mountains of grief
Annoyed by the stars

The stars that cry
Cry upon the Shadow of my Life

End of Spring

I deeply express "I love you no longer"
Maybe I knew
Maybe in spite of myself I knew
Maybe you knew also

The season of our love already gone
It's come to an end you know

All my life, my every breath
Your hands controlled my fears

Continue asking of myself
What am I to do?

Yes, Now this is I who truly speak
What madness, I ask my God

Is it not truth that we should Judge each other?
To Judge our lives together

Our Garden wilting away
Destroyed so by the absence of the tree of Love

By tomorrow, alone I will search
This season of Love is over already
This life of ours seems so still, but yet goes on and on

(Cont'd.)

End of Spring
(Cont'd.)

Such a short season, Oh God!
It's already Winter

Remembering first of spring
When I met you

Never has such a wind come between us
Now the Wind is all around

The Memories

The memories fade away
We continue to hold
Until we once fade also

Memories in our soul continue fading away with time
We all make our mark on Earth

Question is
How long does our mark last?
Once we are gone
Generations continue

Will you remember who I was
My smile, my laughter, my arms, my tears

Will you know my true soul?
My soul that continues through Eternity

Awaken Heart
(for Mr. Michael)

My cheers do not awaken you
The sadness within your soul
I watch while you lay sleeping
Selfishly I ponder such memories

Now that I ask advise from you
As years gone by you gave
I never listen to your voice
A voice with so much to say—

Can you not hear me, I am asking
Awaken somehow the man within
It is not your time to fade, to go
Angry at the timing
Angry at the world—

Awaken the man within
Do not fade away from us
Do you not hear?
We have so much to learn from you

As you sleep uncalmness sets
Uncalmness of your breath
Have you something to say from this
Are we to learn without a speech?

You're suffering I see
So many years gone by
So many years I could have learned
Commanding me to listen

(Cont'd.)

Awaken Heart
(Cont'd.)

But I hear nothing
I sit beside your bed, watching as you sleep

Unsettleness of your Heart
What am I to learn from this?
That pain—oh pain—comes within

So much tragedy among the world
Fight hardest that you're wanted
Fight hardest not to stay

A new day will come soon
Maybe this is "Hell on Earth"
Relax, maybe you're on your way
"Paradise at Last"

Silent Nights

Within the Silent of my nights
I feel an emptiness so intense
A hole within my heart
That no matter can penetrate

An emptiness that deepens
With every passing thought
My joy for life surrounds the empty hole
That neither can penetrate

Oh God, erase the memories
So deep within my soul
Erase the pain so deep
So I can finally let go

America's Heart
9-11

Broken, wounded, hearts that bleed much more
Song of sadness sing so much loudly
Cry, despair, never ending doom

American's Heart Cries
American's Hearts Wounded

We are but one, never to be broken
Together from all despair
Come unite in victory

We mourn for so, so many
Life begins anew
Learn from our past mistakes
Making life a much safer view

The world came out a better place
Of all the destructiveness

We cry today for all the pain
Tomorrow, Sun will shine again

Not beaten down as they so wished
Evil never wins

American's Heart Broken
But our Spirit never dies

(Cont'd.)

America's Heart
(Cont'd.)

Embrace a world of Caring
People come together

Embrace a world of Peace and Love
For all the pain
Births a new life

Together In Much Victory
One Day

Wounded

Oh Peaceful Day, gone away
As two buildings are blown away

People run, People scream
People hurt so badly

Get them, those with not a soul
Grieve for those who walk no more

Sadness in my heart
America is wounded
The World has fallen apart

Will I

Will I ever know the truth
Will it come to me in time
Will it stay beyond my reach?

"Never, ever go back in time"

Will my memories fade from me
Will my life be mine
Will I laugh and sing again?

"Never, ever go back in time"

Will my soul soar anew
Will my heart remember you
Will the memories become scars fading away with time?

Death of Love

I die, Because I Love
A love that hurts so deeply
A wound of many memories
A heart without hope
If I am to speak
Let me die
For my love is too strong
To betray you
My love, I cannot trust
Love may betray you, although
So I die because I love
I love because I die

Surviving

In the midst of such despair
The hell bypasses me
Peace at last comes abide
I'm Free, I'm Free, I'm Free

Memories of a life gone by
I thank the Lord I have survived
Good days make me smile
Yet, bad ones make me cry

I question life so casually
Why, I ask it had to be me

Lifes full of learning ventures
The path of earthly truths

Judgment of our actions
Not wanting to be accused

Knowledge to grow by
Truths to learn from

Not hiding from despair
Attacking head on

Life is still beautiful
Yet, if only it could be shared
Shared with family intact
Family smiles, family cares

Life is a learning venture
God give me credit, I'm surviving

Oh Sweet Sleep

Sleep comes about so still
I can no way unwind
Stone covered thoughts pursue me
My soul so heavy minded
Thoughts of thee unkind

I think of memories of times gone by
With stillness of my heart
Illusions of a thoughtless love
Illusions of a life gone wrong

Sleep comes about so still
I'm no where in my room
Numbness in all the senses appear
Stillness of my sacred womb

Float away and breathe again
Tomorrow comes not soon enough
Sense of worthy memories
Be still my broken heart

Sleep, Sleep, Sleep descends
Follow me once more
Tomorrow brings the light of day
Shining, joyous times begin anew
Unbreak my Broken Heart

My Loss
(for Stella)

My loss so intense
With every soul departing
A part of me disappears

The hole of emptiness exceeds beyond my comprehension
Between my teardrops
Aware that every thing disappears
Sooner or Later
Vanished Forever

My pain intensifies with every bad and good memory
I see no logic in it all
All I know is myself, my ways, my thoughts, my own soul

We are here on earth for just a moment
In the reality of it all
Just a moment in time

Good or bad, drifting about in Life
Some exceeding, some withdrawing
Disappearing as the fog lifts from a dying sunrise

The Sun does appear at times
The Fog always follows

Lost in the memories of it all
Lost in a fog of reality

Reflection of Me

In the eyes of others
A reflection so clear
The ME I've grown to love so well
Is not the ME I found with you

I see myself in many colors
Above the terrace skies
The one I've known for so, so long
The one I have denied

Reflections in others' eyes
Now I see so clearly
Was not myself at all
But my shattered self

Of Lonely Paths

Death be not known to me
Of victims' lonely paths
The road of the existent moments
Erased with every breath
A sacred heart embellished
Into thoughts of no return
A mind creating matters
Leads on to victims own

Prisoner

Prisoner in my mind
Unforeseen time
Withdrawn from the sunshine
Death inside my head

Seeing all that's unreal
Confused by not seeing

Something's wrong again
Never to return
Something's wrong again

Place your picture in my drawer
Never to see again

Need to run to go to hide
Keep my memories of the living

Tomorrow

Tomorrow is a day for me
To be whatever I want to be

Movements of my tired soul
Beckons to come free

Pain within my heart
Keeps me from striving to live

Set me free, Love of Life
Set me free, I pray

Tomorrow is a day for me
My own, my wishes coming true

Live life as it's meant to be
So what's truly right for me?

No Winners

Existing in an empty space
Surrounded by memories of my past
As I imagine life as if
I see nowhere in sight

Oh, where's the victory?
No one wins a war
When evil enters a life
No one wins when ones selfishness
causes others so much pain

Where is the victory?
In all my memories I see no way out
This empty space today I fill with happiness insight

The ones to hold on to, the happy times between the wars
Will erase the sadness

The pain; the pain that although I lived through
My jagged scars still full of pain
Within me eternal blues

Jagged Wounds

Jagged wounds
Amidst the lies

Pieces of my memory lie
Against a bloodied canvas shield
Pieces came together still

Collage of many colors rare
Jagged wounds still sadness, bare

Jagged wounds of open hearts
A wounded heart of bleeding lies

Sweet Baby Emma

An innocence came into my world
Such a beauty of thee unheard

Heavens touch upon the earth
A mass remembrance of all its worth

A cherished smile upon my heart
A look of peace, replaces a broken part

Sweet Baby Emma

Sweetness of your silence
Entices me to smile

Sweetness of your laughter
Stays with me awhile

Sweet Baby Emma

A gift of God's true love
Soft and peaceful as a dove

Broken Places

A shell of emptiness surrounds me
I do not know myself at all
I knew myself years gone by
In the past I knew my mind
Now I'm lost within myself
Someone I never knew before

Acting life's role for me was easy
I played along so well
Now emptiness surrounds me
A shell of silent bliss within

Free me from myself
Free me from my pain
Air surrounds so fresh and free
Just hold on to me

Places of myself familiar
Places I do not know
Gather all the broken pieces
Finally becoming whole

Remembering You

I write this poem
Somehow remembering you
Stay still awhile in time

Do you think of me at all?
Maybe you just cannot show
I reached for you a thousand times

Memories flow so quickly
Perfect pictures in my mind
Do you think of me at all?

Do you see mementos of me
Each and every day and smile
Or push them aside, meaninglessly
And hold your head down with denial

For I choose to remember you
As I first knew you
Hoping you'd remember me as such
How I meant so much
Knowing somewhere, someday, somehow, you'll care

Caribbean Holiday

Moonlight touches my balcony
As the moon shines across the sea

See my reflection so clearly
This is truly me

A paradise of a dream come true
A land of beautiful overflowing smiles

A land of God's graces about
I see myself so free

Magic moments left in time
I never knew this could be mine

The sea, a magical release
The somberness of this moment

So glad to be alive
A break from the maddening world

I love the calmness of the sea
Song of wind and water surrounds me

A song of merriment
I look at life so casually
Now that peace is around me

A melody not written for so long
Chase my tears away

Father's Sons

The father no longer recognizes his own sons
They do not notice their own father

Illusions

Searching the sky for the answers
Forgotten that they had spent some time
The stars on one warm autumn night

Lost

We are so lost in each other
In the grand heart of it all

Gathering all the pieces
Struggling to be whole

Punta Cana

Sunsets outside my window
Beam lights of musical splendor

Breezes overflowing
Surrounds the peace within

A splendid holiday awaiting
A time to start anew

A freshness of the season
The peace I longed for

Moonlight touches my balcony
As the moon shines across the sea

I see myself as I truly am
This is really me

Paradise of a dream come true
I know now how to live

A land of beauty
Overflowing smiles

A land of Gods graces about
I know I'm truly free

Breath

Sunset outside my window
Beam lights of musical splendor

Breezes overflowing scent
Surround the peaceful isle

A peaceful holiday awaits me
A time to start anew

A freshness of the season
Such a clearer view

My Son
(A Momentous Day)

The years gone by
Oh how you've worked

I've never seen before, Integrity of your efforts alone
Shows me how very much you've grown

Hold on my Son, the day draws near
Your actions so sincere

To be revealed as ones true self
Takes so much courage

The pride I hold for you so dear
I give you all my hope, my Love

For life is full of fears
Overcome this and you shall
Become the best you are meant to be

E-Day

I read about you and see your picture
I kiss a thousand times

I see your smile and memories of that smile
From when you were a child
Just lightens up my day

I feel a calmness within my soul
That you are on your way

The knowledge that you've gained this year
Will stay with you a lifetime

Your integrity of your efforts
Have left me completely speechless

I wish you all the luck my love that life can hold for one
That a mother's heart can give

Be content that you have done all that can be done
Trust in God
He holds the Key to your destiny

Keep him near to you
He knows the best

Believe! The road for you is so, so clear

Mother's Soul

She has a soul that embraces all life
Although she herself thinks of death quite often

She worries of the flowers
And the living plants
To water and feed their needs

Although she herself
Is thirsty for freedom
And satisfies none of her own needs

All around her, she makes
All content with Love and Care

But herself a saddened flower
of discontentment

Her thought of her own suffering a secret
False pretence of happiness, protecting those she loves

Protecting them from their own inevitable pain

Time Calls

Darkness in the morning calls
Stay with me much longer

In the midst of equilibrium
I fall to my knees

Sense the mission of my life
Follow to its roots

Morning calls once more
Darkness evaporates

Leaving me with time

Remembrance

In the midst of a family lies
Pieces of unbroken ties
Memories in between
Some not as they seem

Past remembrance of laughter still
Break my heart away
See the days gone by as youth
Capture once this day

Pieces

Pieces of my soul and body
Some touch, existing for tomorrow
Some immense pain for all the sorrow

Laughter heard inside me
Broken all in pieces; never to be the same

Half of me so alive
The other half barely existing

Pieces of my broken heart
Displaced and shattered, falling apart

Immense existence, holding onto pieces

Come together I cry, I shout
For how much longer should I hold out?

Trying to embrace pieces of my heart, my soul
Pieces of my shattered life
Around the broken vessels
Bursting to be healed

Showered me most of all with ecstasy
Surround me more to live with ease

Slowly in my pure existence
I will come together

Whole of me and all of me
Contentment shows again
once more

Lost In My Eyes

We are lost in each other's eyes
In the grand heart of the mountain
Do not struggle for beginnings
Rushing for an old story

Quicksand

As quicksand drawing me down

You took from me my will
You took from me my strength, my world

I find myself removed
Almost unsure

As pavement on an unstable road

I move on
Hold my head high

I am making it; I've survived

As quicksand drawing me down
You tried and tried and tried
I made it to the top—Now My Exit

Sisters

She never thinks about the truth,
She never wonders why

All the memories and all the lies
Make her angry with such defiance

Not wanting to understand
Not wanting to be heard

Such anger in her voice
Such sadness in her soul

I shout to her "Just listen,
Know who I truly am"

All that you ignored in me
All the ME you could not see

Hear me just this once and understand
Just please let me be ME

Midnight Screams

In my mind
There runs a theme

Visions of unfaithful schemes
Haunts me time and time again

In the memories of my youth
Uncles', fathers', husbands' truths

Pieces of that time gone by
Stain my heart
With tears I cry

Someone tell me what was real
Never for my ears to hear

Truth of many years gone by,
No more suffering for the lie

Silent Heart

Quietness whispers to me
As a chill from a faded glacier

I see no need to scream
No one can ever hear

The pain goes through me
As the mark of a blood-stained razor

I speak
I express my true feelings

Hoping one day, somehow, someway
Someone close can hear

Stay Silent My Heart
My soul that bares it all

Stay Silent My Heart
Keep me from the fall

A Needed Love

Come a needed desire
A wish of incompletion

A memory of remission
A thought of pure existence

The memory of my happy days
So unfulfilled in many ways

A wish of complete existence
of unrequired love

A moment left in time alone
A care of unneeded mentions

Alone with thoughts of purity
Pure completion of my life

A love lost over and over
A need to end for once

Oh Jesus

I sing a song of Jesus
His spirit and His love

That fills my heart completely
Touches my soul inside

Holds me from above
He helps me make it right
He makes me whole again

My heart filled with gladness
He takes away all my sadness

Wipe away all my tears
Take away all my fears

Release me from this pain
I pray in Jesus' name

New Hope

In the shadow of despair
I see not wonder where

My days go by so quickly
I'm not one to dare

In the mist of the morning dew
I see not wonder who

Who will come and save me now
From a dreaded place in time.

Save me from my misery I tried to leave behind
In my life with such despair
I see a tunnel of hope shine high

Open up my soul, my mind
I know the happiness I can find
To leave my past behind

Once More

A second chance
Gone out the door

A second chance
To do much more

A dream intent for continuance
No more just a thought in mind

A kind-hearted memory
Left alone
Left behind

A second chance
No more

Existing alone
Look elsewhere to find

Make new memories
Make life to love once more

Remember Me

When I shall leave this earthly dwelling
Go on to Heaven's bliss

Do not shed a tear for me
But only remember this

Remember my heart, my soul, my smile
My poetry that's me

When I am gone
Celebrate with glee

Think of me always and smile
My arms, so gently embracing you

Speak to me always; I'm always around
See my face, my smile, my eyes
In you and your children

When I am gone smile and know
You will see me once again

So live your lives fully
As God intended it to be

Remember me always

(Cont'd.)

Remember Me
(Cont'd.)

For when the wind blows
I will be kissing you

When the trees sway
I will be dancing

And when the sun shines
I will be smiling
So smile as you remember me

Cyprus Sunshine

While the moonlight dances on the glowing sea
The morning dew settles on the glistening sand
This moment of time so touches me

My senses awaken
Remembering you

Your gentle look, gentle ways
Touched my inner soul

You, me in Cyprus
My heart begins to glow

You touched me
My thirst for life renewed

As a rainbow within a settling storm
You colored my world with beauty
You helped me to see so clear

Treasured memories of a lifetime
Magic lights upon a darkened sky

I breathe again knowing
You made me feel alive
Though we see no more of one
I breathe again

I'll take this gift home with me
Laugh and cry at the memory

(cont'd.)

Cyprus Sunshine
(cont'd.)

Your smile touched me for a moment
You have a place in my heart forever

You touched me
And the world became my playground

You touched me
And I feel life again

Island Memories

I take this moment completely in awe
I know now that life is good

Memories of such treasured moments
Such feelings not familiar to me

My soul rejoicing
At such casual peace

Sounds of crystal waters
Drops of sea air embrace me now

Soothes my inner soul
Awakens feelings that are anew

Islands of my dreams
Stay awhile longer
Long enough to heal me

Athens Mist

Fog lifts as a new day awaits me
A misty-covered canvas paradise

An unrecognized land of
Dreams and sunshine coming true

I'm so happy, but still think of you

Thoughts of this new found freedom awakens my soul

Ruined memories fade so quickly
Along with ruined dreams

Islands of ancient ruins of clear turquoise waters
Surround me now

Beauty all about me
Rescuing me from my thoughts

Open Waters

Open Wonders

Serenity, such calmness

I begin to breathe once more

Deep islands of my dreams
Beckon at my door
Rescuing me much more

(Cont'd.)

Athens Mist
(Cont'd.)

At times I do not know what's real

Will I live again?

Will I see again?

Will I embrace this world?
Embrace my life so contently again

Paradise within my heart
Tell me what is real

A journey of such splendid bliss
A life returning that I've missed

Life's Feelings
(Today My Life)

Feelings so intense
We know not what is true
A shattered heart rebelling
A broken soul so blue

Feelings so believable
We act upon their needs
Not meaning to condemn any one
Not meaning to be accused

We sing the song of merriment
Throughout our wondered years
We tear upon the ones we love
Causing them so many tears

To laugh at life so casually
I hide upon request
One thought in mind keeps haunting me
So strong the tie I hold
One thought in mind keeps haunting me
That life is such a Bitter Sweet

Between The Raindrops

Between the raindrops of my mind
Between the life I have denied
Between my most humbling abide

I scream of a life unresolved
I tremble at the lost infinity of my beloved wife
I scream at God for letting me abandon all that was mine

Between the raindrops, feeling safe
Between the empty spaces
I lived life as though I had no tomorrows
Building life among the sorrow

Let me feel the rain, the drops so gently on my face
Cleanse me with your purity

I so afraid to be touched
Afraid to be cleansed
Afraid of healing

Meetings

In the darkness of despair
In the blindness within myself
Falling oh so many times

I have struggled for so long
To find that path
That path that will lead me to that first step
The step that brought me back to you

I feel somewhat like my life's a ladder
So hard, so hard to climb
The top so far away
I've fallen off that step before
But with you I'll fall no more

So help me God to change
Help me and guide me so not to fall again
So I can make it to that second step
And know there's hope again

For Mother

Sometimes my mind just wonders
In a space so unknown
I still can be mistaken
But surely I do know

A life of questioned feelings
A day without despair
No longer have I to wonder
For I shall find it one day

I love for life I once believed in
So fond a tie have I
Believing in tomorrow
Believing have I known

A heart filled with pain
A scared memory of the same
An empty passage of a love undiscovered

I've felt the hurt of so, so many
The pain within their soul
Believing I could change it all
Destroying mine alone

Remembered times of joy
Times I knew not much
Life was heaven then
Have I died and gone elsewhere

Beyond Memories

Beyond the memories of our time
Beyond my existent bonds
I feel for someone so sincerely
That memories pain me deeply

Beyond the magic of such time
Beyond the endless skies
I dream of days gone by afar
Afar that I can't reach them

I cry aloud for such memories
Memories returning
I want from you to replace that hole
That hole I've screamed to feel

Be understanding my love, my life
Be sensitive towards me
If you were I and I were you
I'd be right by your side
To understand, to love, to listen

For I'd always be there for you
So where are you for me?
Where are you?

Love Lessons

Love does not blame nor lie
Love does not criticize
Love holds no remorse
Love has no hatred

Love must heal old wounds
Love must hold dearly those who mean much
Love must make miracles repeat
Love must feel as though you're flying without wings

Love commits positively
Love appreciates differences
Love has beauty to share
Love helps life become a miracle

Love accepts reality
Love, True Love must never be lost

Alone

I am alone, so alone
The earth, my beacon path
The sky, my everlasting space
Yet, I am so alone

Lost on earth
Betrayed by love
Erased all good for me

Life has become a tunnel
Achievement of stubborn moods

A brush, escaping into the past
Wishing death would come at last

Things cannot be the same again
I cannot see the same at all

Waiting to regain myself
Stop the physical gain, I must

Praising God to guide me
It's all I ask
It's all I need

Winter of '98

Into the darkness of the winter
In the silence of my nights

Looking away from my memories
Unto the freshly fallen snow

I am numb
I am lost

Paralyzed with pain
Love only lives within my sleep

Awakening feelings that scare me
Memories that I fear so deep
Numbness from a painful love

I cry
I feel
I hurt

Under the softness of comfort
The fear subsides somewhat

Surrounded by my poetry
Prayers to guide me through

Hiding from this world
My lost life

(Cont'd.)

Winter of '98
(cont'd.)

Despair
Destroyed
Distraught

I feel no life in me
Life can no longer find me

I am numb
I am no longer me

Out of The Darkness
(My Son's Balcony)

I sit on my sons' balcony
I watch the sun setting
Awaiting a new night and a new day coming

I sit on my sons' balcony loving them so
Feeling the fresh breeze, the wind a blow

Awaken my spirit
I thank God I'm alive
I'm almost purely contented, my senses refreshed

My pain and sorrow inside me vanishing so quickly
God, with His gifts, bring me up for a moment with his gentle grace

How can I not be happy once more
The past days so dreary and wicked
I lay on my bed
All wounded and torn

Now that spring's ahead
The Gift that God gave me
Be happy in spirit
Thank God for this moment
This moment of changes

The Most Dearest of Men

(for Jerry Lee)

A man that knew no hatred
A man that never complained
A man having not one bad word to say of another

A man who was completely content
A man of peace and harmony
A man of many happy memories
A man of no regrets

My dearest friend
The ultimate of husbands
The ultimate of fathers
You were truly a Saint on earth

God has placed you by his side as a special angel, I know
May you look down on us from the Heavens
And be our Special Angel below

For a man is like flowers and grass
So flowering in the field of life
A wind so passes quickly
He is gone

Gone to Everlasting Life
Gone to the Heavens

Testament of My Life

Testament of my life
An empty spirit lost
As of a love abandoned
I, such a troubled one
In a troubled world

Painful thoughts within me
A silent limbo so familiar
Embedded so deep within
A Twentieth Century sadden story

Deep the pain as the deepest well
Erasing dreams of the heart
In my life, no longer acquainted

So lengthy is my tragedy
So deepened is my wound
My life hangs on as a wounded bird
Suspended on a stretched out branch

Silent Trap

When memories strike a simple thought
When love seems so unkind
When words alone cannot undo
When life becomes a lie
When truth abides to every word
When two cannot commit
When struggles try to separate
When pain becomes acute
Than alone we must admit
For God believes our every fear
We must fight to save ourselves
Fight to keep our precious gift
Gift of unity and forgiveness

Weapons of The Heart

I look outside my window
I see an open space
A place to breathe contently
A place I can be me

We need the time apart, you know
A time we need to see
If our love is strong enough
To overcome the greed

All I ever wanted was you to look at me
To see who I really am
To see the good we can be

But, other things got in the way
You pushed the love aside
I thought if I could become someone else
You noticed the hurt inside

All it became was ugly
You hated me just more
The tricks used to make it better
Became the weapons that pulled us apart

Them

I just want to let him go
To live the life he wants
Even if I'm glad he's gone
I'm dying so inside

But things cannot be the same
Cause things were never right
What I feel hurts me so
What I know is right

I loved you so
Gave to you
All my life you know
I tried to understand your needs
Until you hurt me so

I do believe in miracles
And if you love me real
Than the time will come my love
When we will be happy still

So go in peace my only friend
Until the day you see
What is really important
If it's them or me

Spring Love

As the birds and the bees sing
As the grass on the ground grows
My love for you will bring
The sun shinning on our souls
For I've thought of love that way
To make life beautiful and to make it gay

Untitled

Oh my dear love
If ever you should think of my feelings
What I want and what I'm bringing
To you, I'll bring my mind, my soul, my life
For you, I'll do what you want me to
For I'm longing to be your wife

Juvenilia
1967-1977

The Cloud of My Soul

I, my whole self when dead,
Shall be reincarnated as a cloud

When thinking over all the times before
All the times I sat wondering about you
Being afraid of losing you

I, out of that great wondering cloud
Shall shed tears of great sadness and gloom

As people see this cloud
Shall think the water coming down is pure white rain

But as you know and I, this water
Is not pure white rain
Not wonderful rain
But are the tears I shed for you
And for my past

So, if ever you see this great cloud
Think of the great sadness and
Gloom that lived within me

Him

To think of him most every day
To look at him and want to say
How much you care
But can not bare
Not to be with him most every day

To get him all alone at last
To make him wonder of the past
That things aren't changed
But must be arranged
For I do feel the same for you
As I hope you do too

He Can Do

If ever a boy comes along
And you know he's all wrong
Well, try to make the best

And try to put your mind at rest
For you can change him
If you want

No more do you have to hunt
For a boy is like a toy
You can find in most any store

To bring him home
And just to find
He'll change
If he's in his right mind

For you, he can do
If he really wants to

Forget You

When will I forget you?
When will my heart be free?

When will I tell myself
This cannot be?

When I can run and go away
From all the people
From this place

Will I forget you?
I ask myself

Will it be over?
Will I be free and gay?

The Listening Wind

Oh, come and talk to me, sweet wind
For there is no one else around
Someone whom I can come out and tell how I feel for one

For one who is so special in my heart
The life of my true soul

I'll tell you all about it
If just you pause awhile

How Lonely

How lonely can one get?
Sorrow follows after happiness
Lonely is the word of one who has lost faith, happiness and love
Loneliness comes through when the word has gone against you
How can one be so lonely?
How can one be so sad?
How can that word of beauty, love and grace be so bad

Anew

As the spring comes again
I see myself begging to gain
A life of cut-out memories and happiness
Which from this, I can't restrain

I'll try so hard to make things better
Because for you I've known the hatred and the bitterness
I've never in my life been like this

So to make you see, I will show
That I will never miss
You

Untitled

To spring and all its loveliness
I confess of all things unspoken
I, for once, have found what I want
And, I for once, have missed
The love I wanted so dearly

Tragedy

Being with you
Something that will never be true

Loving me again
This you can not do

I've never wanted
But now I can't dismiss

Because of you, I know my love
That you will never want it so

And, I will never want the
Tragedy of loving you again

He

He never thinks about the truth
He never wonders why

For he lives in a world of dreams
A world of memories
A life of tears

But wait 'til one day
When he's learned
That life itself
Can change his own

Blue

I think of him most every night
My eyes always full of tears
I ask myself if someday he might
For me, take away all my fears
To love a person as I do
You'd always go to bed
Feeling Blue

No No

Oh, how wonderful it would be
If life was like it used to be
You and me
Me and you
Together loving
Loving together
But now it's dead and gone
Gone and dead
Never to return

This is Me

Born an outsider
From this land
Never knowing where I stand

Always lending a helping hand
But yet, I still don't understand
Why the world today is bad
Why are people always sad

If I could only show how mad I can be
From all this misery

I'd stand up straight and tall
I would
To show the people that I could

And to show them that I must
Be proud to be
To let them see
That this is me
Wondering if I'll ever be free

Native Born

My life is but a simple thing
But has a lot to bring
Born in a native land
Coming over just to see
If it is true
That people here are free
Or are they trapped
Inside their rap
Or are they yet to be

Italy

Listen, my love, to these words of thought from my soul
There is another sun
Another land
Where we can go
Where our souls are free and pure
And we can bloom and die without suffering
My love, I'm wishing a wild desire
For our souls shall live
To word this more smoothly
To tell you all I feel
In my heart, words shall bloom
That the morals of my mouth
Cannot say

Natural Me

My world is made of summer breezes
Walking through the country trees
Being where the air is clean
Shinning with the sun's beam

Nothing But Natural For Me

I love the place where we can rest
Trying to be our very best

Being with our dearest friends
Staying there to the very end

Nothing But Natural For Me

So, as you can see
My life is real
Because I'm free and longing to be
A girl that's brought up proper and right
And always knowing how to be polite

Because it's in me as you know
I've been brought up to show

There's Nothing But Natural For Me

My world is summer breezes
And old blue jeans
Fresh clean air
And the wind in my hair

Nothing But Natural For Me

In a Dream

Sitting here all alone
Wondering if he's my own

In my dreams
He always seems
To be my own forever

But this is real
What I feel

I love him so
Never wanting to let go

To make him show
How much he knows

I'll say and do the things untrue
For there can't be life without you

To a Sweet and Innocent Person

We have felt for life that all shall be
Be real to you and me

To see the things unspoken of
To believe the truth in me

For it's said that can be said
And all will be the same

In years to come
With all its fun

We will live to be
To follow the sun

To follow such a precious thing
To know that it will bring

Sunshine and happiness to your life
To bring you back into this life

For life is what the world is now
For life shall teach us how and why

Untitled

Now he knows how I feel
How I love when he is near

When my body feels free
Just for him to touch me

For to me he is so dear
He'd be my life, my love, my dreams
If only things would only seem
Like a dream that's coming true
Because, for you I'd be true
If I could only believe in you

True Feelings

Such a feeling I had in me
A feeling that was truly real

We laughed and played together
We lay upon my bed

I thought, that in my head
That I began to live again
but now there's only pain

It came so quickly and so gentle
And now it's gone forever

Like a winter storm that hits so quickly
Then it settles down

Now your love has gone quickly
But will I ever settle down
Or will my life keep going on like a winter storm

Leaving Madness

Leaving this land
Knowing I might never come back
Seeing all the things I've had
Crying over things that made me sad
I, for once, am glad
For this place is mad

A Lovely Loneliness

Will I come back again
Or will I stay?

Will I see your lovely married loneliness?
Will I stop, talk or just walk right by?

I have often wondered
What I would do

So for years we'll wait and see
If you're still around

That Boy

Just beside the table I saw
A boy with anger, heartache and all

Not because no one has liked
But because of what he is like

He's the kind of boy that gives a damn
But cares enough for a helping hand

Sometimes he's quiet
Sometimes he's not

This is what makes him
Hard to forget

Easy, Simple and Sweet

To make it easy, simple and sweet
To make those heartaches not repeat

I'd like for you to pause awhile
To listen to my sorrow, anguish and smiles

I'll write this so to let you know
You've hurt me so
I just can't let go

You've driven me to madness
You've driven me to sadness
And now it's all over

So High

Being high above
In a space never ending
Loving the free movement
The air, so much of it
Loving the never ending feeling of life
Moving around
Being all over
Free, so free, so very, very free
Every movement so new
Every thought so clear
Every touch so simple
Everyone so real

I Too

Of all the reality of sinners
I, too, am one

Existing to be known
Trying all of kinds
Missing so many times

Never planning my world
Living for little things
That should mean more

I am the sinner of all kind
Feeling everyone has my mind

Me, being a part of all people's thoughts
I am the reality of the sinner
For I have done it too

I Am You

I am the universe
And of all things existing
I come from

Beneath the surface of the sky
I too exist
Along with the stars, moon and sun

I am the universe
The being of reality and sin
Of all things
I am of thee

Among all natures beauty
I, too, am surviving
The trees, fields and gardens

With all we are one
Races of the golden crown

Being all one
In a universe beneath the sky

Feelings of Love

I am from the skies beautiful thoughts
Nature's reality of life

I am from the earth's flowered fields
I remove, if only betrayed

Being beautiful for all
If living only to please and satisfy

I love the world of every imaginary feeling coming true
For this gentle feeling to me
Is the love I hold for you

My Blood

The blood in my veins beat a tune of sadness
That no one else can hear
But when you're near to touch my breast
The blood in my veins
Then shall rest

Wondering All

How can such a thing be true?
Something I've treasured all year through

I cared and treated so very kind
Starting to think is was all on my mind

But now the truth has all come out
What could I do but fight
I prayed to my God, my Heavenly Father
To make all things turn out right

For I did pray to have it this way
So I can turn and just say
It happened in the past
Back on that day

For when its over and done
I can rest and have my fun
So things will turn out right for me
I deserve the best of things because I am me

For also all the pain
I've caused you mother
We need a break for life this way

So I can fully live out each day
And make things better for you all the way
For to get rid of such pain like this

I'll pray and pray each day
For He shall hear me and say
That He'll be with me
          All the way!

Lost Love

I've seen the moon and the stars shine above
But yet, I have not found my love
I've known the rivers and the seas
Not yet, have I ever been free
You wonder why I'm doing this
It's because I, for once, have missed
The love I thought so free and gay
But now it's over
Never again to stay

In Love

I am the world's golden touch
I am the thing that means so much
You and I
I and you
In the world just for two
A world where love is what matters
A world where caring is so fair
So great is our existence
In a world made for two
Two in love

My Stars

Sweet star of love
So fond am I
For such a joyous tie

A tie which had flown from I to you
Because I've wished upon you once
Wondering what you really are

You did make my wish come true
For you took my thoughts that made be blue
You made me realize what to do

Now that I have loved and learned
Learned and loved
All the thanks goes to you

Unknown

(Poem to Live by)

After awhile you learn the difference
Between holding a hand and chaining a soul
And, you learn that love doesn't mean security

You begin to learn that kisses aren't contracts
And presents aren't promises
You begin to accept your defeats
With your heart and eyes wide open,
With the grace of a woman,
Not the grief of a child

And, you learn to build all your roads on today
Because tomorrow's ground
Is too uncertain for plans,
And futures have a way of falling in mid-flight!

After awhile you learn that even
Sunshine burns if you get too much
So you plant your own garden, and
Decorate your own soul instead of
Waiting for someone to bring you flowers.

And, you learn that you really are strong
And, you really do have worth

And, you learn and learn
With every goodbye
And letting go, you learn!

"Forgiveness is the sacred aroma of ones soul that sweeps its sweet essence about life in airs of adversity."

Natalina Russo

Index of First Lines

Printed in the United States
212065BV00001B/7/P